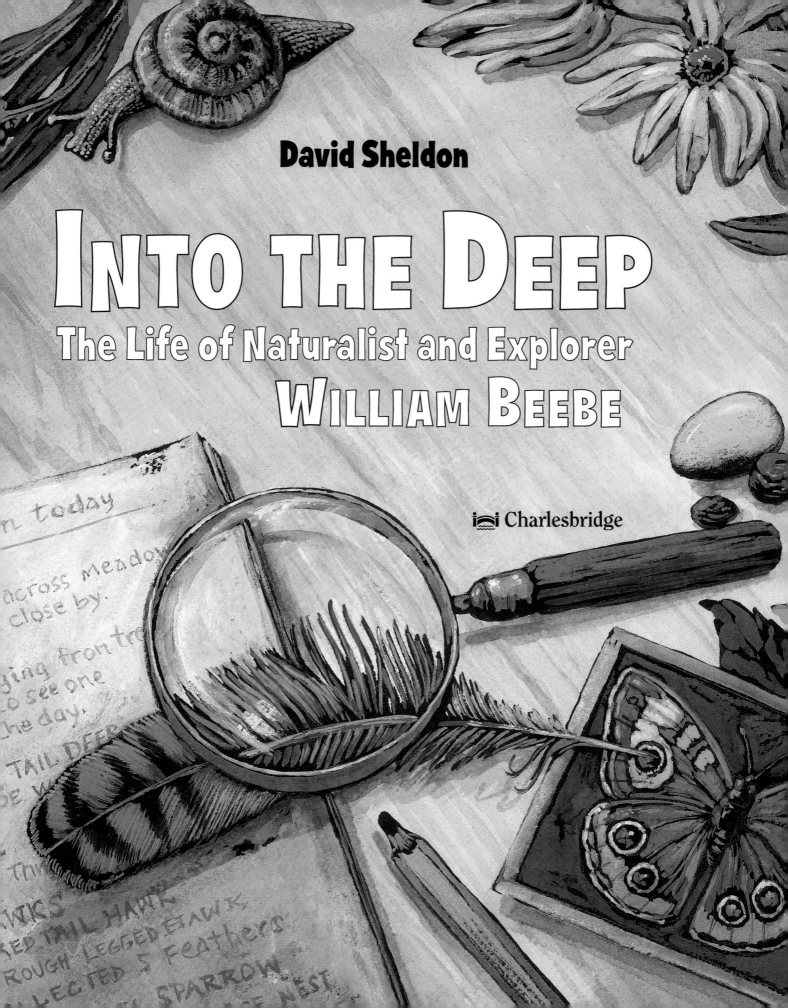

David Sheldon

INTO THE DEEP
The Life of Naturalist and Explorer
WILLIAM BEEBE

Charlesbridge

To fearless explorers
William, Sarah, and Christopher

Published by Charlesbridge
85 Main Street, Watertown, MA 02472
(617) 926-0329 • www.charlesbridge.com

Library of Congress Cataloging-in-Publication Data
Sheldon, David.
   Into the deep : the life of naturalist and explorer
William Beebe / David Sheldon.
      p. cm.
   ISBN 978-1-58089-341-1 (reinforced for library use)
   ISBN 978-1-58089-342-8 (softcover)
   ISBN 978-1-60734-215-1 (ebook pdf)
1. Beebe, William, 1877–1962—Juvenile literature. 2. Zoologists—
Biography—Juvenile literature. 3. Explorers—Biography—Juvenile
literature. I. Title.
QL31.B37S44 2009
508.092—dc22   2008025341
[B]

Printed in Korea
(hc) 10 9 8 7 6 5 4 3 2 1
(sc) 10 9 8 7 6 5

Illustrations done in acrylic, gouache, and India ink
   on 140-pound cold press watercolor paper
Display type and text type set in Animated Gothic and Adobe Garamond
Color separations by Chroma Graphics, Singapore
Printed by Sung In Printing in Gunpo-Si, Kyonggi-Do, Korea
Production supervision by Brian G. Walker
Designed by Susan Mallory Sherman

Born in 1877 in Brooklyn, New York, William Beebe was an only child whose parents cherished him. His parents were both nature lovers. Wanting to encourage Will's own love of nature, they decided to move to rural East Orange, New Jersey.

Will spent every moment he could exploring the hills and streams near his family home, studying and collecting animals. He wanted to become a naturalist.

He trained himself to move slowly and quietly through the woods like his hero, the Native American warrior Uncas from *The Last of the Mohicans.* By the time he was twelve, Will was an expert animal tracker.

On brisk autumn days Will and his mom counted
migrating birds. The annual migration count was started by
the Audubon Society as a way to track how many birds
move through different parts of the world each season.
Birders across the country count the number of each species
and report back to the society, which continues to log the
data to this day. Birds fascinated Will, and he participated
in the migration counts all his life.

One summer day Will's father found a young owl,
its parents nowhere to be found. Will named it Moses and
raised it all by himself. Moses was always interested in Will's
latest find—though maybe not in the same way that Will was!

With all his collecting, Will's bedroom became a small natural history museum. Will taught himself taxidermy and displayed his stuffed birds. He had aquariums filled with fish and some with snakes. He mounted countless insect specimens. He also had plant and rock collections. He wrote in his field journal, "To be a naturalist is better than to be a king."

By the time Will was eighteen, his passion had become his profession. His articles on nature appeared in newspapers and magazines. Before Will had even graduated from college, he was hired by W. T. Hornaday, director of the New York Zoological Park, to be the assistant curator of birds. He cared for the park's birds and gathered new specimens.

Soon Will was traveling the world on scientific expeditions.
As a member of the New York Zoological Society, he explored
dangerous and remote areas of Mexico, South America,
and Southeast Asia in search of rare species of birds and
other animals.

The world in Will's day was very different from the world we know today. Large parts of the earth's land, seas, and skies were still unexplored, with countless animals yet to be discovered.

In his travels Will realized that collecting animals and bringing them back to museums and zoos was an outdated method of study. He was one of the first naturalists to attempt the often risky approach of observing animals in their natural habitat. He would stake out an area of jungle and study it from top to bottom. Will's method of studying nature made him a pioneer in what we now call the science of ecology.

Will wrote books about his explorations that captured the public's imagination. His adventures made him a household name. A wealthy admirer even gave Will the use of a large steamship called the *Arcturus,* which came with its own research laboratory.

For his next adventure, he traveled to the Galápagos Islands, where Charles Darwin had made the observations that led to his famous theories of evolution. He wanted to continue Darwin's study of the island's unusual inhabitants, such as the marine iguanas.

While in the Galápagos, Will tried helmet diving for the first time. He was amazed by the variety of life he discovered underwater. The experience convinced him to devote the rest of his life to studying and exploring the ocean and its creatures.

Will continued his ocean studies off the island of Bermuda.
His team of scientists lowered nets into the water to catch
sea creatures. Unfortunately, many of the delicate creatures
from the deep seas fell apart when they were pulled up to
the surface.

Frustrated, he decided it was time to try something that no one had ever attempted. He would visit the creatures of the deep in their own environment. Now he just needed a way to get there!

In 1928 Will teamed up with an engineering student named Otis Barton. Otis was as excited about exploring the ocean depths as Will. He designed a deep-sea diving vessel, which Will named the Bathysphere.

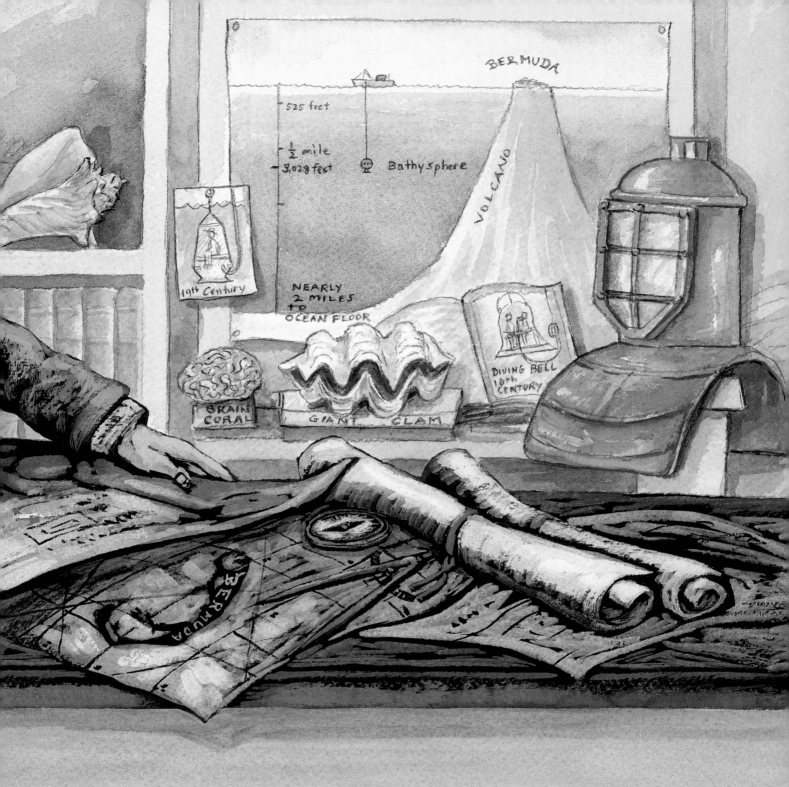

Plans were made for the first ever deep-sea expedition.
Both men would need plenty of courage for what they
were about to do. No one before them had descended more
than 525 feet below the ocean's surface and lived to tell
about it, but Will and Otis planned to go even deeper!

The two-and-a-half-ton Bathysphere was created in a hot, steamy foundry in New Jersey. Its walls were made from one and a half inches of thick steel. Many unmanned test dives were necessary before the men could ride in it.

On one test the Bathysphere came up filled with seawater because of a small leak. If Will and Otis had been inside, they would have drowned. The hatch shot out like a bullet from the force of the pressurized water inside. Fortunately no one was standing in the way!

Will and Otis began a series of manned dives in June of 1930. Finally, on August 15, 1934, they were ready to attempt the deepest dive ever made. With Will and Otis huddled inside, the Bathysphere was lifted over the rolling waves of the Atlantic Ocean. Through his headset Will gave the order to the communications officer, Miss Gloria Hollister: "Lower the Bathysphere!"

The Bathysphere was plunged into a different world. Clouds of foam and bubbles gave way to an awesome view. The ocean surface above them undulated like a waving magic carpet. Daylight streaked down in great shafts of light as in a cathedral.

The Bathysphere slowly descended from the world of
sunshine and warmth into one of midnight blues and
unbearable coldness. Will gazed at the vibrant ecosystem in
action: squid and fish fed upon small shrimps and snails,
which in turn fed upon even smaller plankton.

As they descended into the abyss, Will was startled by an enormous creature gliding by them in the darkness. "It must be at least twenty feet long!" he gasped.

It was impossible to identify the mysterious sea monster. The explorers were nervous, but continued their journey.

A half mile (2,640 feet) down, Will felt as if he were in outer space. In the pitch-black water, eerie creatures with fantastic shapes emitted their own light. The Bathysphere continued to descend as far as its cable would reach—a record-breaking 3,028 feet. Once again Will's explorations made him a pioneer. His underwater journey opened up a new branch of scientific research into the deep seas.

As years passed and the earth's frontiers were explored and studied, Will changed his focus once again. He saw that every creature, from the biggest to the smallest, was important to the earth and needed protection.

Through his writing and lectures, he promoted conservation and struggled to help save the earth's vanishing wilderness and endangered animal species.

During his final years Will returned to the study of his beloved birds. He opened a research station on the island of Trinidad. From time to time, aspiring young explorers and scientists visited, eager to show the friendly scientist their latest finds from the jungle. To this day scientists continue to be inspired by Will's work.

Diving Deeper into the Story

In 1895 the New York Zoological Society and the New York Zoological Park (now the Bronx Zoo) were established by President Theodore Roosevelt and other prominent men as part of a plan to preserve America's wilderness and animal life. In 1899 William Beebe (pronounced BEE-bee) began his career as assistant curator and soon was responsible for the care of all the birds at the park. His enthusiasm, drive, and writing skills soon won him many admirers and benefactors, including Roosevelt himself.

In 1916 Will established a research station in British Guiana (later Guyana). It was here that he developed his unique method of direct observation of animal behavior. Will's books, the first of which was released in 1918, were scientifically groundbreaking and enjoyable to read. They contributed to the public's understanding and appreciation of the natural world.

NBC aired a live broadcast of one of the Bathysphere's dives in 1932. Reeling from the Great Depression, Americans were hungry for heroes. They sat riveted to their radios as Will gave them an audio tour of a new and exciting world. He became a celebrity and used his fame to his advantage by urging people to care for and respect nature.

In 1952 Will officially retired after more than fifty years of research. In his lifetime he discovered many species of animals. His favorite research subjects included the primitive hoatzin bird, three-toed sloth, and ghost butterfly—all native to the deep jungle—as well as the lantern fish and anglerfish of the deep seas. Will's adventures continue to inspire new generations of scientists, and his books are still read today.

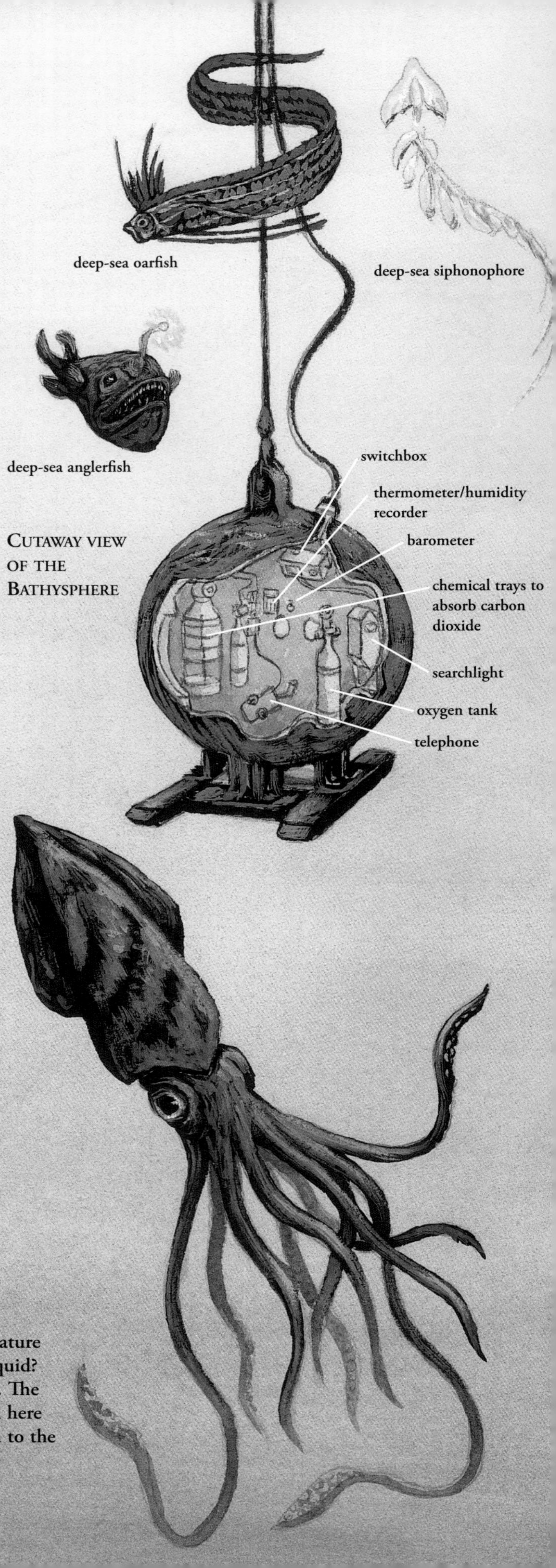

deep-sea oarfish

deep-sea siphonophore

deep-sea anglerfish

CUTAWAY VIEW OF THE BATHYSPHERE

switchbox

thermometer/humidity recorder

barometer

chemical trays to absorb carbon dioxide

searchlight

oxygen tank

telephone

Was the mysterious creature that Will saw a giant squid? No one knows for sure. The size of the squid shown here is in correct proportion to the size of the Bathyspere.

"To be a naturalist is better than to be a king."***

and other quotes by William Beebe

*Beebe's journal, December 31, 1893

"When I first entered the majestic jungle of Guyana I forgot to keep on the alert for danger because I felt so completely at home."—*Half Mile Down*

"When you look for things . . . year after year, and train your senses to concentrate, then sooner or later very special things happen within sight or hearing."
—*Nonsuch: Land of Water*

". . . I am deep down under the water in a place where no human being has ever been before; it is one of the greatest moments in my whole life!"—*The Arcturus Adventure*

"I can only think of one experience which might exceed in interest a few hours spent underwater, and that would be a journey to Mars."—*The Arcturus Adventure*

"[There is] one fundamental reality in wild nature—the universal acceptance of opportunity—evolution has left no chink or crevice unfilled, no probability untried, no possibility unachieved."—*Edge of the Jungle*

". . . when the last individual of a race of living things breathes no more, another Heaven and another Earth must pass before such a one can be again."—*The Bird, Its Form and Function*

Glossary

Bathysphere: From Greek words that mean "sphere of the deep." A steel ocean-diving vessel that can be lowered by cable to great depths.

conservation: The careful use and protection of natural areas to prevent the loss or injury of plants and animals.

curator: The person in charge of a zoo or museum or a department therein.

ecology: The branch of biology dealing with the relationship between animals and their environment.

endangered: Something that is in danger. An *endangered animal* is threatened with extinction by natural and/or man-made causes.

environment: The surroundings in which an animal or plant lives.

evolution: A scientific theory stating that all currently existing plants and animals were developed from similar species that existed in the past.

habitat: A place where a particular animal or plant lives and grows.

migration: The movement of animals from one location to another during the changing of the seasons.

naturalist: A scientist who studies nature.

taxidermy: The skill of preparing, stuffing, and mounting an animal skin for display.

Resources

Beebe, William. *The Arcturus Adventure: An Account of the New York Zoological Society's First Oceanographic Expedition.* New York: Putnam, 1926.

Beebe, William. *Half Mile Down.* New York: Harcourt, Brace & Co., 1934.

Beebe, William. "A Half Mile Down," *National Geographic,* December 1934, 66.

Beebe, William. *Jungle Peace.* New York: H. Holt, 1918.

Gould, Carol Grant. *The Remarkable Life of William Beebe: Explorer and Naturalist.* Washington, DC: Island Press/Shearwater Books, 2004.

Matsen, Bradford. *Descent: The Heroic Discovery of the Abyss.* New York: Pantheon Books, 2005.

Matsen, Bradford. *The Incredible Record-Setting Deep-Sea Dive of the Bathysphere.* Berkeley Heights, NJ: Enslow Publishers, 2003.